THEN & NOW®

NEW HAVEN

This is a *c.* 1930 view looking east down Broadway.

THEN & NOW®

NEW HAVEN

Colin M. Caplan

ARCADIA
PUBLISHING

Published by Arcadia Publishing
Charleston, South Carolina

Printed in the United States of America

Then and Now is a registered trademark and is used under license from
Salamander Books Limited

Library of Congress Catalog Card Number: 2006923199

For all general information contact Arcadia Publishing at:
Telephone 843-853-2070
Fax 843-853-0044
E-mail sales@arcadiapublishing.com
For customer service and orders:
Toll-Free 1-888-313-2665

Visit us on the Internet at www.arcadiapublishing.com

This is a *c.* 1930 view of the Fair Haven neighborhood looking north on Ferry Street toward the corner of Wolcott Street.

CONTENTS

Acknowledgments

Special thanks to Francine, Bob, Amy, Guru Dev, Henry, Wayne Chorney, John DeTulio, and Sheba. Thank you, God.

United Advertising Corporation

SUCCESSORS TO

The New Haven Sign Co.
The New Haven Poster Advertising Co.
The Bridgeport Outdoor Advertising Co.

OUTDOOR ADVERTISING
THROUGHOUT CONNECTICUT

Commercial Signs

Electric Signs

Office, 833-843 State Street

New Haven, Conn.

New York City   **Newark, N. J.**   **Bridgeport, Conn.**   **Dallas, Tex.**

Above is United Advertising Corporation's advertisement in the 1917 directory, their first year in New Haven.

INTRODUCTION

Then & Now: *New Haven* will never really show what the city looks like now but will always be a series of moments caught through the camera's lens. So perhaps this is a book of thens, showing physical and cultural changes that have occurred over the last century. I could only come to this conclusion when I began searching for the corresponding present-day views, and I realized that there are many people and projects on the move. Attempting to capture a static view of urban and population change may have been too great of a challenge, but a number of key issues come to light through this portrait.

One major question lingers in my mind that defines the human experience as it relates to living in an urban environment, sharing space with others, creating territorial boundaries, and spreading our boundaries past the threshold of what we need: What happened in New Haven where economic disparity, unemployment, youth violence, and land abuse seem to have replaced the city's once glorious cultural heritage? That is not to say that nothing great has come out of the city in the last 50 years, but this question could be asked of numerous urban areas around the country. In comparing the then and now portraits of New Haven, the most obvious surveillance is the physical deterioration of the pedestrian-scaled environment that catered to the simple convenience of living, working, and shopping in a relatively small area.

The elements that inspired a certain density and activity in New Haven related to the forces of mobility and access needed to provide for and sustain a family. If the Puritans from England settled to pursue a mercantile city free of their king's restrictions, then the influx of immigrants arriving in waves from various countries of Europe followed a similar pattern. The many groups that immigrated to the city came for employment opportunities that either did not exist where they were from, or they were escaping environments with escalating social and economic problems.

The influx of southern African Americans and Puerto Ricans beginning in the middle of the 20th century was also born by the desire for a better lifestyle. New Haven was the land of opportunities until the manufacturing employment base left the city after World War II ended. Combining this force with inexpensive, race-restricted real estate opening in the surrounding suburbs, New Haven's decline was in full force.

Redevelopment under Mayor Richard C. Lee during the 1950s and 1960s deurbanized many of the commercial districts and dispersed thousands of people whose homes were in the way. This was followed by increasing disparity between nurtured institutions and the communities that became increasingly underrepresented. The protests for equal treatment in the Hill neighborhood followed by the 1967 riots signified real problems in what was supposed to be a "model city."

Today's New Haven is characterized by two major institutions, Yale University and Yale-New Haven Hospital, supplying much of the culture, services, and employment to the region. The downtown has seen a new vibrancy based on new upscale housing and restaurants, but that energy has not spread to all of the neighborhoods. There are semblances of revitalized community spirit in many neighborhoods that will be the key factors to the city's future success in attracting stable investment and a sense of place and pride.

The collection of historic images represented in this book were taken by the United Advertising Corporation in order to show their clients and creditors how their billboards and signs could be seen by the average pedestrian. I purchased the collection from an antique dealer who revealed to me that his seller found them next to a dumpster. The images are mostly original negatives with many original prints as well. The film types range from Kodak 116, 117, 120, 122, and 35 millimeter and range in age from 1918 to around 1970.

Prior to United Advertising Corporation working in New Haven, there existed a small number of billposters. Way back in 1857, Col. Lewis E. Blakeslee began a billposting business that eventually would be called the New Haven Bill Post Company in 1897. In 1914, the business changed its name to both the New Haven Sign Company and New Haven Poster Advertising Company, moving to 833 State Street.

In 1917, the United Advertising Corporation, headquartered in New York City, took over this local advertising operation, and in 1918, Leonard Dreyfuss, then company vice president living in New York, wrote *An Idea that Saved a Business* about United Advertising Corporation's merger of 10 national advertising companies. In 1926, Art Sign was started by Arthur Birchman, and it became affiliated with United Advertising, and in 1940, they moved to 190 Whalley Avenue. They ran the business there until a new building was constructed for them at 119 Water Street in 1967. The company expanded its services under the titles United Electrical Contractors and Canterbury Realty Company, which purchased and maintained sites for billboards.

The process that allowed United Advertising to create large posters with rendered images and words began with artists drawing a small version. That work was then photographed, developed, and enlarged into a slide. The slide was used to project the image onto large sheets of paper where artists traced the images, coloring and filling as needed. The sheets were removed and brought to the site where they were unrolled and posted onto a board with an adhesive.

Intensely used and experiencing numerous changes and shifts over the last 90 years, downtown was once marked by numerous large department stores, local banks, and countless small shops and restaurants. Downtown began its decline as a shopping center just about the time that the *c.* 1945 image below was taken, showing the southwest corner of Temple and Crown Streets. The tower on the left-hand side marks the old United Illuminating headquarters, built in 1938 and designed by local architect Roy W. Foote.

Chapter 1

DOWNTOWN

This was probably one of the busiest corners throughout New Haven's history due to its connection to the water, railroad, and businesses. Looking up State Street at the corner of George, Fleet, and Fair Streets, the image above from 1922 shows how dense and varied this corner of downtown was. On the far right-hand side was Andrea Cimino's fruit and produce shop, which only operated here for one year. The larger four-story building across the street housed the Hotel Venezia and Napoli Rooms, both offering furnished rooms for the recent Italian immigrants. The image to the left shows the effects of urban redevelopment.

Cities are always in a state of flux, which can change with the blink of an eye. This view looking east down George Street toward Orange Street has been the site of numerous renewals and redevelopments. The image below, from 1921, shows a heavily used street filled with carts and cars buying, selling, and trading various goods. The present view to the right will soon look very different after the planned implosion of the Veteran's Memorial Coliseum with its weighty four-story parking deck on the right-hand side of the image. The Coliseum was completed in 1972 and designed by local architectural firm Kevin Roche John Dinkeloo and Associates as part of the a major redevelopment program begun in the 1950s.

The bank on the busy corner of Church and Crown Streets has changed little since the photograph above was taken around 1935. Built in 1906 for the Connecticut Savings Bank, the building replaced the Second Empire–style Hoadley Building, which was destroyed by fire in 1904. The bank was built at the height of the Beaux-Arts movement in architecture and was inspired by the Erechtheum on the Acropolis in Athens, Greece. Looking past the bank, the four- and five-story buildings housed offices, stores, hotels, and Chamberlain's furniture store at the corner. The image on the left shows that a parking lot to the rear of the bank has replaced all of the buildings between the bank and the Chamberlain building.

This view of the corner of State and Elm Streets is no longer the busy center of activity it was when the image below was taken in 1921. Many of the shops here were longtime fixtures like the Deegan-Hope Drug Company, operated by Joseph Deegan and Frank Hope. State Street was one of the city's main business thoroughfares, and it was lined with three- and four-story mixed-use buildings. This and the following view show the effects of redevelopment on the urban fabric and how the removal of the street wall creates less reason for a passerby to shop, eat, or activate along the street.

This view demonstrates some of the effects of large-scale urban redevelopment and street-widening the cityscape. The image above dates from around 1922 and shows the busy scene at the intersection of Grand Avenue, State and Elm Streets, looking west. The entire east side of State Street was razed and paved by 1980 as part of a redevelopment plan to ease traffic and parking. The heavy hand of the bulldozer resulted in the decay of the street as a shopping destination. The image on the left shows the wide horizon from the bridge over the rail line.

History repeats itself along this stretch of Church Street looking north toward the Green, the historic marketplace. The *c.* 1925 image to the right shows the busy scene of restaurants, offices, and banks with the county courthouse, built in 1909 and designed by local architectural firm Allen and Williams, in the background. The image below shows the former Chapel Square Mall, built in 1965 to draw shoppers away from the street, which replaced two densely built city blocks. The mall is now converted to upscale apartments and shops facing the street on the ground floor.

This view looking south down Church Street toward Chapel Street has always been the center of town. The Green is at the right-hand side along with the monument-like Benedict Fountain, built in 1909 and designed by John Ferguson Weir. The image above, from around 1925, shows the six-story Second Empire–style Gamble Desmond Insurance Building, built in 1871, beyond the Green. The image on the left shows that many of the buildings on Church Street still exist, including the former Second National Bank, built in 1913, on the far left-hand side.

Long the home of Michaels Jewelers, the southwest corner of Chapel and Temple Streets has seen a number of changes. The image below, from around 1925, shows the building that was originally built as a hotel and called the Kenwick House. In 1941, the art moderne–style building incorporating curved glass windows replaced the old hotel. The image to the right shows this building now housing a Subway sandwich franchise. Irving Michaels moved his family's business to New Haven in 1915. Although they moved out of the city, Michaels has chain stores throughout the state.

This view down Temple Street south toward Crown Street shows the redevelopment era's drastic changes to the streetscape. The image to the left, from around 1948, gives an idea of the amount of activity that took place downtown. The sign on the right-hand side would soon read the Paramount Theater, which was built as the Olympia in 1914. In 1973, the theater was replaced with the present three-story office building as seen in the image below. The inundating horizontal structure on the left-hand side is the Temple Street Garage, built in 1961 and designed by Paul Rudolph.

This is a view of Elm Street looking west toward Orange Street. In the image below, dating from 1950, the facade of Benedict Memorial Presbyterian Church is visible on the far left-hand side. The domed tower of the Union Trust Building still remains a beacon in the center of the image. The large building across on the left side of the image to the right was built for the New Haven Savings Bank in 1972 and was designed by local architect William F. Peterson. The area is still regarded as a center for lending institutions.

The demand for parking has had a detrimental effect on the city's streetscape, as seen in this view of Orange Street looking south toward Elm Street. The image above dates from July 1949, and the building with the storefront on the left-hand side was the original location of Harold's formal wear. Harold's is named for Harold Pellegrino, who began the store in 1946 with siblings Al and Evelyn. Although they have moved around the corner to Elm Street, Harold still runs the successful store.

The corner of the old Arena rink can be seen on the far left-hand side of the image below, dating from 1941. The building in the foreground was the Orange Grove Garage, appropriately named for being of the southwest corner of Orange and Grove Streets. The garage was operated by Henry Paschetto and Hans Olsen until 1942, when the Southern New England Telephone Company purchased it for its vehicles. Southern New England Telephone replaced the garage with the present building in 1967, as seen in the image on the right. One improvement made to the building in the last five years was the addition of a few windows and some trellislike appendages.

Looking south down Whitney Avenue from the corner of Audubon Street around 1935, the small rise in the street is due to a bridge originally built for the Farmington Canal. The canal began in 1828 and ceased in 1947, when the New Haven and Northampton Railroad laid tracks on the old canal bed. Redevelopment in the late 1980s and early 1990s created a new dense urban neighborhood that centered around the area's connection to offices and the arts. The tall office building on the left-hand side of the image to the left replaced the old Century Building in 1990 and was designed by local architectural firm Cesar Pelli and Associates.

Restaurants, shops, theaters, and parking have been staples along this stretch of College Street, looking south from directly in front of the Shubert Theater. The theater's entrance was through the Hotel Taft Annex at the far left-hand side of the image below, taken in 1933. The tall building on the right-hand side was the Hutchinson Apartments, built in 1893 and demolished in 1933 for a parking lot. At the end of the street was the Zunder School, built in 1895 and named for Maier Zunder, a local civic and business leader and an early member of the city's Jewish community. Although the school was demolished in 1954 for a parking lot, the image to the right shows how the street was extended in 1957 during redevelopment.

The redevelopment era created sterile streetscapes, as seen in this view of George Street looking east from York Street. Block-long stretches of limited-use buildings replaced the houses, stores, and apartments that provided daily use of street-level spaces. The image above, from April 1949, was taken about five years before the neighborhood was razed. The fence on the left-hand side with the Star of David marked the entrance to B'nai Jacob Synagogue, which was torn down in 1962. The structure that replaced it is the parking garage for Crown Tower, which was built in 1965.

As its name indicates, Broadway is a wide street created by the confluence of roads heading north and west. The image below, from around 1920, looking east toward York Street, shows its strip of businesses on the left-hand side that have continued to play an important role in the area. Its proximity and appeal to Yale's students has lead the university to purchase the buildings along Broadway. The image to the right shows the two-story infill building with three facades built in 2001 by the university to draw national chain stores.

On May 28, 1938, the 300th anniversary of New Haven's founding, the 2nd Company Governor's Foot Guard led one of the grandest parades through the city. The image above shows the grand marshal, Col. Charles E. Lockhart, in the lead in front of the crowd at Broadway, Tower Parkway, Whalley Avenue, and Howe Street. The spectators that day were estimated at 20,000. Much of the open paved area is now part of a public parking lot and landscaped traffic islands, as seen in the image on the left.

This view shows the edge of the Broadway shopping district at the corner of York Square Place, around 1935. Looking west toward Goffe Street, the image below shows the stores on the right-hand side that were cleared for Yale University's Morse and Stiles Colleges, built in 1960 and designed by Eero Saarinen. York Square, which was located a block down York Square Place on the right-hand side of the image, was originally designed with stately Greek Revival–style mansions in the early 19th century and then became home to the city's three high schools. In the 1920s, Tower Parkway carved through the square and is the large intersection in the image to the right.

Yale University students mingle and make their way to classes in the above photograph of Sterling Memorial Library through the grand courtyard of Cross Campus around 1940. The library was built in 1927 and designed by James Gamble Rogers in the neo-Gothic style. The small tower on its roof is part of a miniature model of the Yale campus. Built in 1933, the Cross Campus buildings, flanking both sides of the image, were also designed by Rogers. The image on the left shows that besides the clothing fashion, not much has changed in this view.

The Oak Street neighborhood was once one of the most culturally diverse and populated areas of the city, located south of downtown. To the south, the Hill, named Sodom Hill and Mount Pleasant for the rise along Davenport Avenue, absorbed many of Oak Street's middle class. The Irish, African Americans, and Germans were some of the earliest immigrants followed by Eastern European Jews, Italians, Armenians, Lithuanians, Greeks and Poles, Southern blacks, and Puerto Ricans. The *c.* 1925 image below shows West Water Street looking north from the corner of Portsea Street near Union Station.

Chapter 2
OAK STREET AND THE HILL

This view shows the center of a once bustling shopping district called Congress Square. The image above dates from around 1930 and is looking south from Church Street down Congress Avenue. The four-story building on the left-hand side of the image was the Price and Lee Company, publishers of regional city directories, which burned down in 1957 while it was awaiting demolition due to redevelopment. After the Oak Street Connector was built here, Church Street was extended south, as shown in the image on the left. The building on the left-hand side is the headquarters of the Knights of Columbus, built in 1967 and designed by Kevin Roche John Dinkeloo and Associates.

Looking north up Congress Avenue toward downtown from the corner of Liberty Street, much has changed since the *c.* 1925 photograph below. Congress Avenue was the commercial heart of the Hill neighborhood, with the streetcar line attracting dense development. The image to the right shows how redevelopment from the mid-1950s to the 1970s affected the streetscape and decimated the once thriving shopping district. The building on the right-hand side of the street is the John B. Pierce Laboratory, built in 1933.

The photograph above from around 1930, looking east up Congress Avenue from the corner of Vernon Street, shows the density of buildings and stores that once lined the street. Just beyond the corner structure on the left-hand side, in a four-story brick building, the Mounds candy bar was first made by the Peter Paul Candy Manufacturing Company in 1921. The tall building down on the right-hand side of the street was built in 1924 and designed by local architect Roy W. Foote. Converted into a nurses' dormitory by Grace Hospital in 1928, the building was replaced by the Anlyan Center for Medical Research, built in 2003 and designed by Robert Venturi, as seen in the image on the left.

The city's largest institutions, while needing to provide greater services and expand their physical domain, often take over or destroy their surrounding neighborhoods. This can be seen clearly in this view of the northwest corner of Howard and Congress Avenues. The image below dates from around 1948 and shows the shops, apartments, and houses that bordered the city's major hospital, then called Grace-New Haven Community Hospital. In 1995, Yale University built the garage pictured in the image to the right to support the hospital and medical school. The hospital's trend of expansion into the neighborhood continues well beyond this block.

This view is of the corner of Congress Avenue and White Street, looking south. In the image above, from around 1930, the Direct Importing Store was located in the corner building. The store catered to the neighborhood's large Italian population and was operated by Andrew Sacco, who lived upstairs. Although the building on the far left-hand side still exists, the image on the left shows how redevelopment due to blight and cultural shifts has changed the area. The shops and apartments were replaced by the Redevelopment Agency with low-density apartments and houses based on suburban models.

Congress Avenue's shops provided Hill residents with items for their daily needs prior to redevelopment in the second half of the 20th century. This image below shows the corner of West Street looking east, around 1930, with numerous storefronts mixed with housing. The sign for ice cream on the corner building on the right-hand side of the image was Alfonso Carusi's confection shop. Carusi lived down the block on West Street. In the image on the right, the corner building is one of the few still standing, and it now houses Ring One Boxing, a center for training city youth in boxing and instilling in them a sense of purpose and hope.

Fast moving cars, sterile buildings, and walls are some of the results of the redevelopment of the Oak Street area. This view east up Oak Street from the corner of Broad Street shows the transformation of a once lively neighborhood. The image above, from around 1940, hints at the complex array of businesses and tenements for which the area was known. George Goldberg's pharmacy on the left-hand corner and the Russian Baths on the right-hand side of the street catered to the neighborhood's Jewish population. In stark contrast, the image to the left gives no reminder of the old neighborhood.

No longer a street, the view north up Davenport Avenue at the corner of Oak and Broad Streets leaves nothing to the imagination. Only the memory is left of James Como's shoe repair shop on the right-hand side of the photograph below from 1925. This entire block was razed for the Yale School of Medicine's Institute of Human Relations, built in 1926. The building in the foreground with arched windows is the Yale Child Study Center and was added in 1999, designed by the local firm Centerbrook Architects. Note the prancing frog sculpture in the garden below.

Oak Street was largely dominated by small shops and apartments prior to redevelopment in the 1960s. Looking east from the corner of Asylum Street around 1930, the photograph above shows Chepovsky's Deli and Grocery. The shop was run by Isadore Chepovsky, and he employed his family members Barnett and Hyman as clerks. The surrounding neighborhood was largely Jewish at this time. In the photograph to the left, the entire block is now the site of the Hill Regional Career High School, built in 1998 and designed by the local firm Architects Environmental Collaborative.

This part of Oak Street was renamed Legion Avenue in 1928 in honor of the American Legion. The photograph below, from around 1930, is looking west down Oak Street at the corner of Orchard Street. The Weibel Brewing Company was on the left-hand side of the street, and the building on the far left-hand side was the brewery's bottling house, built in 1913. On the far right-hand side was the Elm City Meat Market owned by David Miller. Miller lived in a house just behind the store. The image on the right shows the neighborhood's devastation after redevelopment.

Looking north up South Orange Street in the photograph above, from around 1930, this was once a busy commercial district. The street was partially created from Commerce Street in 1921 as part of a master plan to connect downtown with Union Station. The building on the far left-hand side of the image was built as the Derby Passenger Railroad in 1871 and later became the railroad employees' YMCA. The tall building on the right-hand side was the Kilfeather Building, built in 1920 to house films for the motion picture industry. Both buildings were razed in 1957 to make way for the Oak Street Connector. On the left-hand side of the image to the left are Tower East and Tower One, built in 1969 and designed by Charles Moore Associates.

This area has been New Haven's center of transportation since the original Union Station was built here in 1875. The *c.* 1930 photograph below is looking north up Union Avenue and shows, on the right-hand side, the Union Station built in 1918 after fire destroyed the earlier one. The station was designed by Cass Gilbert and is the largest railroad station between Boston and New York. The image to the right shows the station still existing, but the entire surrounding area has been redeveloped over the years.

This view is looking west from the head of Columbus Avenue at Union Avenue around 1932. The building at the far right-hand side in the image above was the Hotel Garde, named after Bill Garde of Waterbury in 1914. Situated on Columbus Avenue, U.S. 1, and across the street from the railroad station, the Hotel Garde was one of the city's largest hotels. Among the many famous people who stayed here, the Garde hosted Eleanor Roosevelt on April 28, 1936, for a speech on labor. The image on the left shows a completely changed scene with a number of streets closed or skewed, executed after redevelopment in the 1960s.

Horse-drawn wagons persisted in New Haven into the 1930s, as shown in the below image from around 1930. Looking north up Howard Avenue from the corner of Gilbert Street, the brick building with horizontal stripes on the left-hand side of the image was the firehouse housing Engine Company 1 and Hook and Ladder Truck Company 2. The building was built in 1881 and designed by local architect Rufus Russell. The two, five-story buildings in the distance on the right-hand side of the street were the Sarah Wey Tompkins Surgical Pavilion, built in 1932, and the Raleigh Fitkin Memorial Pavilion, built in 1932. Both pavilions are part of Yale-New Haven Hospital and exist today with additions, as seen in the photograph on the right.

Looking north up Cedar Street at the corner of Spring Street, the photograph above is from around 1930. The store on the right-hand side, rear corner, was Louis and Ida Levinson's ice-cream store. They lived in an apartment behind the store along with another family member, Herman Levinson, who was the manager. The image to the left shows the scene today with many of the structures remaining. This area of the Hill is the Trowbridge Square neighborhood and is adjacent to the railroad tracks.

This view shows the head of Kimberly Avenue, looking north from Lamberton Street to Howard Avenue. The image below dates from around 1930 and shows the cluster of shops at the confluence of the roads. The large utility pole at the center of the image marks where the New York railroad line passes under the road. Like many of the Hill's business districts, the real estate in this area has faced a physical decline but manages to serve some of the neighborhood's vital needs. The image on the right shows some of the effects of these changes.

Kimberly Square is on the right-hand side of this view of Lamberton Street, looking east from the corner of Kimberly Avenue. The photograph above is from around 1930, when the square, actually a small triangle, was known as Prohibition Square. Lamberton Street is named for George Lamberton, who was one of the city's earliest settlers and merchants. It was his ship that sailed away in 1646 never to return, but it was claimed that a ghost ship was seen in the clouds. The image on the left shows that the intersection still retains its cluster of storefronts.

The Wooster Square neighborhood, east of downtown, was originally a center of maritime trade in the late 18th century, called the New Township, and then became known as the carriage manufacturing center of the world by the mid-19th century. Early African American and Irish communities began here, followed by Bavarian Jews, Poles, Swedes, and, most prominently, Italians. The *c.* 1925 photograph below is looking east on Wooster Street, from near the railroad cut, bordering the ancient path of the East Creek.

Chapter 3

GRAND AVENUE AND WOOSTER SQUARE

Grand Avenue was one of the principal commercial streets radiating out of downtown. Lined with furniture shops, groceries, clothiers, and tenements, the avenue prospered while home to numerous immigrant communities. This view is looking west at the corner of Jefferson Street showing, in the photograph above from 1920, the corner building called Alderman's Block and built in 1894. Jewish immigrants had settled on Grand Avenue in two waves, first in the 1840s and then in the 1890s, with many stores representing their community. Only a vestige of the old buildings remain today on this part of the avenue.

Grand Avenue was the main street with all types of stores, multiple movie theaters, and churches. Looking east from the corner of Franklin Street, the photograph below, from around 1927, shows a full cultural experience. The corner drugstore was run by Louis Montanaro, representing the Italian community that had its center in this area. Located next door with the large awning was the Dreamland Theater, which opened in 1926. The tall steeple in the background was St. Patrick's Roman Catholic Church, which was founded by the burgeoning Irish community. The entire neighborhood was demolished during and after the construction of Interstate 91.

These photographs are looking east down Grand Avenue from the corner of Wallace Street. The image above dates from around 1930 and shows that the avenue was a continuous stretch of stores and apartments that resembles little of what the area looks like today. Grand Avenue in this part is now sterile, deserted, and lacking any reason for a person on foot to stop here. It is hard to imagine now that there could have been a time when this corner was brimming with neighbors mingling and having a bite to eat.

Looking east on Grand Avenue from the railroad crossing, the Mill River bridge is just up ahead. The bridge was originally built in 1793 and called both Bell Lane and the Barnsville Bridge. The photograph below dates from around 1920 and shows the highly industrialized uses along the river. On the far left-hand side of the image is a sign for Pasquale Cusano's Italian bakery, which he ran downstairs from his apartment. The large three-and-a-half-story building toward the center of the image still exists in the image on the right although the top floor and a half have been removed.

This view features what was the heart of the Wooster Square neighborhood, looking west up Chapel Street at the corner of Franklin Street. In the image above, from around 1930, the tall building in the background burned down in 1960, while the rest of the buildings in the image above were razed for the Conte School. The school was built in 1960, designed by Skidmore, Owings and Merrill, and can be seen in the right-hand side of the image on the left. Interstate 91, which cleared the entire width of a city block, runs just behind the view.

This was the center of New Haven's 19th-century carriage manufacturing industry. Looking east down Chapel Street toward Wallace Street, the area once housed up to 20 carriage body and parts factories. The *c.* 1930 photograph below shows the M. Armstrong and Company carriage, and later automobile, manufacturers in the five-story building in the center. By the time this photograph was taken, their business had folded, like many similar plants in the city. Ironically, the building now houses a bicycle sales and repair shop, perhaps the carriages of the 21st century.

This view looks south down East Street from the corner of Chapel Street toward the harbor. East Street was an industrial axis along with houses and apartments. The *c.* 1942 image above was taken around the time when manufacturing was beginning to decline in the city. Within 20 years, the city redeveloped the entire neighborhood through highway construction and by demolishing 90 percent of the buildings. Although a couple of buildings were spared, seen in the photograph to the left, the area is now mostly a sea of sprawling parking lots.

W ater Street allowed access to New Haven's harbor, and merchants built houses on the street early on. But by the mid-19th century, the port's industrial and commercial demands changed the street into a grittier environment. This view is looking west from the corner of Warren Street. The photograph below dates from around 1928 and shows Casper Barney's tavern on the far right-hand side. After redevelopment and the construction of the Oak Street Connector, located just to the left of the photograph to the right, new buildings were erected, and a number of streets were closed. The tall building on the right-hand side was built in 1963 and designed by local architect Carleton Granbery. A building located just out of the picture on the right-hand side was the home of United Advertising from 1967 until they closed.

New Haven's connection to its port was no better displayed than on Water Street. The view looking west toward Brown Street in the image above, dating from around 1930, shows a variety of buildings related to storing, processing, and distributing goods, particularly lumber, traded on the wharves. The entire south side of the street was removed for the connector, and more land was created by filling a corner of the harbor. Water Street now bears little connection to its past and is overshadowed by the highway overpasses and ramps.

State Street was called Neck Lane, and it led north to a bridge over the Mill River, giving access to Fair Haven and on to Middletown. An early West Indian blacks community began along the street followed by Italians and Poles. State Street was the only commercial thoroughfare through the East Rock community and is the best preserved commercial avenue left in the city. The photograph on this page is looking at the northeast corner of State Street and Middletown Avenue, from February 1949.

Chapter 4

STATE STREET AND EAST ROCK

Downtown used to meld with the East Rock neighborhood on State Street at this point looking south at the corner of Bradley Street. The photograph above, from around 1930, shows the businesses and apartments that were wiped out by the Trumbull Street Connector to Interstate 91. The insertion of the overpass creates an urban dead zone that creates a visual and psychological separation of the streetscape. The image on the left demonstrates how unappealing the corner is when it continuously casts a shadow and creates a cavelike space.

State Street is one of the few commercial thoroughfares in the city that has not been completely redeveloped into a suburban model. These photographs are looking north at the corner of Summer Street, located in an area that has been one of the centers of the Polish community. The view below, from around 1920, shows that variety of stores and houses that gave the street its ethnic flare. Although Summer Street is just a driveway and the corner building has been a bit overly sided, the street largely remains as it was.

This was the center of the United Advertising Corporation's universe in New Haven until 1940. The photographs are looking south at the corner of State and Franklin Streets. In the above image, from around 1930, the building that straddles the corner behind the signs was the company's headquarters, starting when it was called the New Haven Sign Company. When the highway was built, Franklin Street was cut off, and in 1976, the corner building was replaced with Central Veterinary Hospital. The spire in the background on the right-hand side is St. Stanislaus Roman Catholic Church, the first church built by the Polish community in 1913.

This is the southwest corner of State and Humphrey Streets where some slight alterations have occurred. The buildings on the left-hand side of the street in the *c.* 1930 photograph below were part of the Hygienic Ice Company. Now the corner building houses a donut shop. The filling stations on the corner are in the same location, but the site has been expanded farther down State Street. The biggest change to note is the presence of traffic lights instead of a police officer standing on a platform in the middle of the intersection.

The confluence of State, Humphrey, and Hamilton Streets created a large triangular intersection called Humphrey Square. The *c.* 1922 photograph above shows the square looking east down Humphrey Street toward Joselyn Square, marked by a group of trees in the right-hand side of the image. Note the horse drinking from the basin. Now marked by Interstate 91, Humphrey Square has become a parking lot, as seen in the photograph on the left. Joselyn Square is now tucked away in a remnant neighborhood isolated by the highway, railroad, and Mill River.

The scene looking south on State Street from the corner of Edwards Street is still recognizable in the image below, dating from around 1930. Almost every building on both sides of the streets still exist. Joseph Deegan, who ran the pharmacy on the far right-hand corner, also ran the Deegan-Hope Drug Company at the other end of State Street at the corner of Elm Street (page 13). By the early 1980s, the area was mostly abandoned and awaiting redevelopment until a number of businesses began to open. Now the street thrives with restaurants, shops, offices, and apartments, and open parking spots are often difficult to find.

State Street straddles Interstate 91, which crosses the street here at the Mill River. This view is looking west at the bend in the road. The bridge was the site of the first crossing over the Mill River, called the Neck Bridge from the earliest days due to its connection to the Fair Haven peninsula, or neck. The image above dates from 1925, when the area was clustered with manufacturing plants, garages, and houses. This was where the Cedar Hill neighborhood began before the highway removed a number of city blocks. A major part of redevelopment in New Haven focused on highway construction clearing swaths of densely populated blocks and relocating people to other neighborhoods and towns.

Dixwell Avenue has been the center of the black community for over a century. The street runs northwest out of downtown, and the neighborhoods that developed around it became some of the poorest by the 1830s, one section being called Poverty Square. Newhallville was heavily developed after the Winchester Repeating Arms Company built its factory on Winchester Avenue in the 1870s, and it provided housing for immigrants from Ireland, Germany, and eastern Europe. The *c.* 1925 photograph on this page is looking north up Dixwell Avenue from the corner of Webster Street.

Chapter 5

DIXWELL AVENUE AND NEWHALLVILLE

Dixwell Avenue was named for John Dixwell, one of the regicide judges who fled from England after sentencing Charles I to death. This view is looking south toward Broadway from the corner of Bristol Street. Although the street was largely a commercial thoroughfare, the view above from around 1930 shows that there were a number of houses as well. Dixwell Avenue has continuously been the target of urban redevelopment projects, which have greatly affected the streetscape.

Redevelopment can remove or replace the identity and sense of place from an area, as shown in this view of Dixwell Avenue and Foote Street looking south. The below photograph from 1928 shows numerous stores to purchase daily needs. The one-story building on the corner in the center of the image was the People's Meat Market run by Harry Chadloff and Samuel Fried, who catered to the small Jewish community in the Dixwell neighborhood. The image on the right shows the buildings that replaced the city's first low-income housing project called Elm Haven, built in 1939. The new project is called Monterey Place, named after a mid-20th-century jazz club where famous acts played.

The story of Dixwell Avenue is deeply tied to the black community who built numerous houses of worship, operated stores and restaurants, and dwelled here. The above photograph from around 1940, looking south on Dixwell Avenue at the corner of Charles Street, shows the steps to one of the few remaining historic churches on the far right-hand side. Varick Memorial African Methodist Episcopal Zion Church was built here in 1908 and in 1915 was the site of Booker T. Washington's last public speech. Every other building in the image was razed during redevelopment and replaced by 1968.

These photographs are looking south on Dixwell Avenue from the corner of Admiral Street, one block north of the previous image. The below view, from around 1922, shows the street during its most active commercial growth. The three-story brick building on the left-hand side was clearly built as an addition on the front of an older house. This was a common practice that allowed the owner to gain both commercial and residential space to rent. In the image to the right, the four-story building on the far left-hand side corner was built in 1993 by the Hannah Gray Home, expanding this 145-year-old institution for senior African American women.

This view is looking south on Dixwell Avenue from the corner of Henry Street, again one block north of the previous page. The c. 1930 photograph above shows the commercial importance of this street to the community, with every house having a storefront addition built on to the front. When the brick buildings at the corner were built, the house that was located on that site was moved to the rear, shown on the far left-hand side. In 1965, at the height of Dixwell Avenue's redevelopment, the corner buildings were replaced by Trinity Temple of God in Christ Church, seen in the photograph on the left.

Winchester Avenue was named for the Winchester Repeating Arms Company, which was founded here by Oliver Winchester in 1866. This view with the factory in the background is looking north at the corner of Munson Street. The *c.* 1940 image below shows the plant near its peak size when it covered more than 81 acres of floor space and was the largest employer in the city. Many of the plant's surviving buildings are vacant after the company merged and downsized into a new facility. The buildings in the background are now awaiting a future occupant as part of Science Park, a start-up site for growing biotechnology companies.

This scene shows what happened to the manufacturing jobs in New Haven in the second half of the 20th century, looking north onto Winchester Avenue at the corner of Munson Street, site of the original plant. The photograph above, from around 1935, shows the hustle and bustle of workers heading for a lunch break. The Winchester plant was the main influence to the growth of the Newhallville neighborhood throughout the late 19th and early 20th centuries. The photograph on the left shows the vast postindustrial landscape that left its neighborhood without its major source of employment.

The toll on a neighborhood for losing its major employment base is poverty, depression, and then blight. This view of Winchester Avenue and Lilac Street is looking south toward the Winchester plant. The area is named Newhallville for George T. Newhall's carriage factory from around 1850, built along the New Haven and Northampton Railroad line, which ran through the area. The below photograph, from around 1930, shows the neighborhood's vibrancy while the image on the right shows the physical decay. The buildings are presently owned by the city, awaiting the probable demolition claw of redevelopment.

This view looking north up Shelton Avenue toward the corner of Thompson Street has been completely redeveloped. The above photograph shows the street around 1930, when it was in the center of Newhallville's industrial activity and was lined with shops and apartments. Like many of the area's commercial streets, it physically declined after the loss of the manufacturing job base. The image on the left shows the apartments built in 1980 on three of the surrounding blocks.

Starting just west of Yale University, the Dwight neighborhood was an early center for the carriage industry and was an early center of the African American community. The area developed slowly westward until the 1890s when middle-class housing supplied homes for, among others, Greek and Ukrainian immigrants. Whalley Avenue became highly commercialized in the 1920s when automobile dealerships settled and expanded. The image on this page shows Chapel Street looking west at the corner of Kensington Street from around 1925.

Chapter 6
WHALLEY AVENUE AND DWIGHT

Dwight was once called the West Village, and Park Street was the heart of its carriage manufacturing. The street has become the western border of Yale's campus, although the university is slowly expanding its territory into the Dwight neighborhood. The photograph above, from 1927, shows the view looking south from the corner of Elm Street with automobile dealerships and repair shops that existed before the university built Davenport College. The college, on the left-hand side of the image to the left, was built in 1933 and designed by James Gamble Rogers.

New Haven's nickname, the Elm City, rings brilliantly in this photograph of George Street looking east from the corner of Day Street. The image below dates from 1923, when Rose Halper ran a grocery store in front of her apartment on the left-hand side corner. In 1925, the three-story Beverly Apartments replaced the older wooden structure as seen in the photograph to the right. Apartment houses like this sprang up throughout the city during the 1920s due to the demand for increased apartments and the high land value.

These photographs are looking east down Elm Street from the corner of Orchard Street. The image above dates from 1925 and shows the corner store on the right-hand side that serviced the neighbors' needs. The area's first significant residential development began in the 1840s with small frame houses built by carriage assembly workers and artisans. Then large Victorian-style homes were built by company owners and businessmen. By the time of this photograph, three-story tenements and apartment flats existed alongside. Many of the buildings on the right-hand side remain today although altered in appearance.

The corner of Norton and Chapel Streets was the place to catch the streetcar until they were removed from service in 1948. Looking east down Chapel Street, the photograph below, from around 1949, captures some of the stores that marketed their services to those in transit. Even after the streetcar route was discontinued, the corner showed liveliness with large signs and advertisements. Although still housing stores on the ground floor, the same building today with its blank wall lacks the eye-catching appeal. The comparison is an excellent example of how sterile and unattractive a building can become with its details shorn, its windows closed, and its identity masked by vacuity.

Looking north onto Norton Street at the corner of Derby Avenue, this is now the West River neighborhood due to its proximity to the river. The image above from 1921 shows Frederick Brothers meat and grocery on the right-hand corner run by Edward and Henry. Edward's son, Edward Jr., was listed as a musician in 1926, ironically the same year that the widowed mother of Arthur Arshawsky, better known as Artie Shaw, moved across the street. On the site of the old grocery store, the image below shows the Yale Bowl Wine and Spirits appealing to football fans who pass this corner on their way to a game.

Whalley Avenue has been an important thoroughfare for the western part of the city since it was incorporated as part of the Litchfield Turnpike in 1797. This view, at the corner of Orchard Street looking east, shows the dramatic shift the avenue has taken. The *c.* 1930 photograph below shows the graceful elm trees lining the street in front of substantial homes on the left-hand side, but it also shows the intrusion of commercial establishments, particularly automobile related, that began the change to a major commercial district. Mostly lined with fast food chains, liquor stores, and pawn shops, the construction of a supermarket, seen on the right side of the image on the right, was hailed as a major success. United Advertising was located in a building on this block from 1940 to 1967.

This view west up Whalley Avenue looking toward the corner of Hobart Street is a couple blocks from the author's home. The photograph above dates from 1933, when this stretch was considered the outskirts of town. The small groceries, bakeries, delicatessens, and pharmacies were built in response to the needs of surrounding middle-class residential developments. In the image on the left, the local Laundromat, Chinese takeout, and dollar store represent the current trend in the neighborhood's taste.

Fair Haven, once called Dragon after the sunning seals on the shore, was a separate township until 1870. The first settlers began building fishing and oystering shacks on the west side of the Quinnipiac River. Westville, once called Hotchkisstown, was a separate village for many years prior to becoming a part of the city of New Haven in 1872. Both sections remained fairly isolated geographically from the rest of the city until the Fair Haven and Westville Horse Railroad began operation. The *c.* 1928 photograph below shows Grand Avenue looking east at the corner of Ferry Street in Fair Haven.

Chapter 7

FAIR HAVEN AND WESTVILLE

This view on Grand Avenue looking east from the Mill River into Fair Haven shows one of the largest industrial sections of the city. The photograph above, from around 1930, shows numerous smokestacks from the old English Station Power Plant built on a man-made island in 1899. Although the building is still there, it sits vacant. The image on the left shows a Quonset hut, a rare metal frame structure from the World War II era, on the right-hand side.

Grand Avenue is Fair Haven's main street lined with stores and apartments. This view is looking west from the corner of Lloyd Street, showing the densely built business block. The photograph below, from 1924, shows a storefront addition being added to M. Frank Hope's drugstore. This section was home to a large Italian community. The area is now the center of the Latino and Puerto Rican community, as evidenced by the numerous signs in Spanish in the image on the right.

Chapel Street in Fair Haven experienced industrial development in the late 19th century and, soon after, residential development with the influx of workers and immigrants. The view looking east down Chapel Street toward Lloyd Street shows the changes that have happened since the manufacturing plants closed. The image above is from around 1935 and shows the gritty scene of tenements, stores, and foundries. The street today lacks the urban density that gave it a sense of purpose.

Straddling Fair Haven in its middle, Ferry Street is a principal road leading north and south of the peninsula and was named for the path to the ferry that crossed the Quinnipiac River. This view is looking north toward the corner of Chatham Street with Snake Rock, a hill next to East Rock, rising behind the trees in the background. In the *c.* 1925 photograph below, the corner building on the right-hand side is having a storefront addition completed. The store was opened by Andrew Tasso, who lived upstairs, for a grocery. Now the corner is occupied by a large wing of what was once the Saga-Lou dairy products company, as seen in the image on the right.

Fair Haven was once called the oyster capital of the world due to the harbor's mudflats and the ability to process the prized cuisine. This view looking south on the Quinnipiac River from the Grand Avenue bridge shows the oysterman's wharves that became prime spots for machine shops, coal storage, and eventually metal scrap yards. The photograph above, from around 1930, shows the array of wharf buildings in various stages of disrepair. The spire on the right-hand side belongs to the East Pearl Street Methodist Church, built in 1871. The image on the left shows the park and townhouses constructed after successive redevelopments.

Forbes Avenue was named for the Forbes family, who lived along this road, east of the Quinnipiac River. The photograph below, from around 1930, was taken at the corner of Stiles Street looking east. The building on the far right-hand side is the Church of the Epiphany, built in 1904. The two-story house next to it is Jehiel Forbes's house and dates from 1767. When the British attacked the city in 1779, the house was the victim of shelling from a ship. Until the recent past, the cannon ball was still lodged in the side wall. Although these two buildings are still extant, most of the neighborhood has been paved over or rebuilt.

The Annex section of the city, taken away from East Haven, had its center in this photograph of Townsend Avenue and Main Street. Looking north, the *c.* 1925 photograph above shows an extremely quiet scene. The intersection was called Four Corners and is now completely obliterated by the highway. With more lanes in construction now, the sunken Interstate 95 is sunken below street level to reveal the far block. The church on the corner is St. Andrews Methodist Church, built in 1892.

Joseph Abramovitz must have appreciated the Ritz cracker advertisement enticing customers to his grocery store next door, shown in the photograph below from around 1938. The view is looking down Whalley Avenue toward the corner of West Rock Avenue. The image on the right shows the A-Won Deli and Grocery in the same building. Interestingly, the author purchased all of the historic images in this book in the building just past the three-story apartment house. At the time, it was Wayne Chorney's antiques store and is now being renovated by John Cavaliere, antiques dealer and talented guilder.

The center of Westville along Whalley Avenue has long been a commercial district. The photograph above from 1930 is looking east toward Edgewood Park. The men in the street appear to be marking a spot where a hole was to be dug. The intersection on the right-hand side was the spot of numerous taverns, including Morse's Tavern, also known as the Elm Tree Inn, which was built on that site in the mid-18th century. Although the tavern was torn down in 1909, the two-story building on the right-hand side of the image on the left was for many years the home of the Cape Codder Restaurant and now houses Delaney's, a popular evening spot and restaurant.

Not far from the end of the streetcar line, this view of Whalley Avenue looking west at the corner of Dayton Street shows the growth of the street's commercial presence. The image below dates from 1924, when the one-story brick building in the center of the image was being built for Arthur J. Smith's drugstore. With the Parker Paper plant located directly across the street off of the right-hand side, a cluster of stores served the population of workers. The image on the right shows the effects of numerous alterations to the brick building.

The bucolic nature of New Haven's surroundings is shown clearly in this photograph of West Rock ridge in the Amity section of Westville. The view is looking west from the corner of Amity Road and Litchfield Turnpike, which shows the rural landscape in the image above from around 1925. The effects of population growth and commercial sprawl have severely changed this view. West Rock, part of the second-largest state park, is a bastion of nature with rare species and isolated ecosystems. The dip on the right-hand side of the ridge, called Wintergreen Notch, was part of the Paugussett Trail, a major route between precolonial native villages.

The people involved with selling and making the signs are the unseen forces guiding this book. Generations have gone by since the photograph below, from around 1950, was taken of Art Sign employees, who were affiliated with United Advertising. They are, from left to right, (first row) unidentified, Harry DiLeonardo, Jerry Coppolla, and Ed Holman; (second row) Harry Blondell, Walter "Wonder Boy" Blackal, Earl "The Pearl," unidentified, Buss Carroll, and unidentified. Some of today's employees of Sign-Lite, started by former Art Sign employee John DeTulio, are, from left to right, Gabor Stein, Fran Liseski, Mike Romanchick, Rick Heller, Paul Mone, Dave Esposito, Mark DeTulio, Elaine

DeTulio, Eric Johnson, Bob St. John, Sheryl Gleason, Diane DeVincentis, and Paul Hoffman.

Bibliography

Balzer, Richard. *Street Time*. New York: Grossman Publishers, 1972.

Brown, Elizabeth Mills. *New Haven: A Guide to Architecture & Urban Design*. New Haven, CT: Yale University Press, 1976.

Cannelli, Antonio. *La Colonia Italiana di New Haven*. New Haven, CT: Stabilimento Tipografico A. Cannelli Company, 1921.

Dammann, George H. *75 Years of Chevrolet*. Sarasota, FL: Crestline Publishing Company, 1986.

Flammang, James M., and David L. Lewis. *Ford Chronicle*. Lincolnwood, IL: Publications International Ltd., 1992.

Herman, Barry E. *Jews in New Haven Volume II*. Hamden, CT: Abbott Printing Company, 1979.

Holden, Reuben A. *Yale: A Pictorial History*. New Haven, CT: Yale University Press, 1967.

Hornstein, Harold, John O. C. McCrillis, and Richard Hegel. *New Haven Celebrates the Bicentennial*. New Haven, CT: Eastern Press, 1976.

http://www.laborhistory.org/index.html

Lattanzi, Dr. Robert M. *Oyster Village to Melting Pot: The Hill Section of New Haven*. Chester, CT: Pattaconk Brook Publications, 2000.

Leeney, Robert J. Elms. *Arms & Ivy: New Haven in the Twentieth Century*. Montgomery, AL: Community Communications, 2000.

Maynard, Preston, ed., Marjorie B. Noyes, ed., Sylvia M. Garfield, associate ed., and Carolyn C. Cooper, associate ed. *Carriages and Clocks, Corsets and Locks: The Rise and Fall of an Industrial City—New Haven, Connecticut*. Hanover, NH: University Press of New England, 2004.

Murphy, Wendy. *A Leader of Substance: Yale-New Haven Hospital at 175 Years*. Lyme, CT: Greenwich Publishing Group, 2001.

New Haven Directory. New Haven, CT: Price and Lee Company and J. H. Benham, 1857-1970.

Rae, Douglas W. *City: Urbanism and Its End*. New Haven, CT: Yale University Press, 2003.

Sarna, Jonathan D. *Jews in New Haven*. West Haven, CT: Kramer Printing Company, 1990.

Shumway, Floyd, and Richard Hegel. *New Haven: An Illustrated History*. Windsor Publications U.S.A., 1987.

Starr, Harris. *Elwood Second Company Governor's Foot Guard Souvenir History*. New Haven, CT: M. H. Davidson Company, 1950.

Stewart, Daniel Y. *Black New Haven*. New Haven, CT: Advocate Press, 1977.

Townshend, Doris B. *Fair Haven: A Journey Through Time*. New Haven, CT: Eastern Press, 1978.

Townshend, Doris B. *The Streets of New Haven: The Origin of Their Names*. New Haven, CT: New Haven Colony Historical Society, 1984.

Warner, Robert Austin. *New Haven Negroes: A Social History*. New Haven, CT: Yale University Press, 1940.